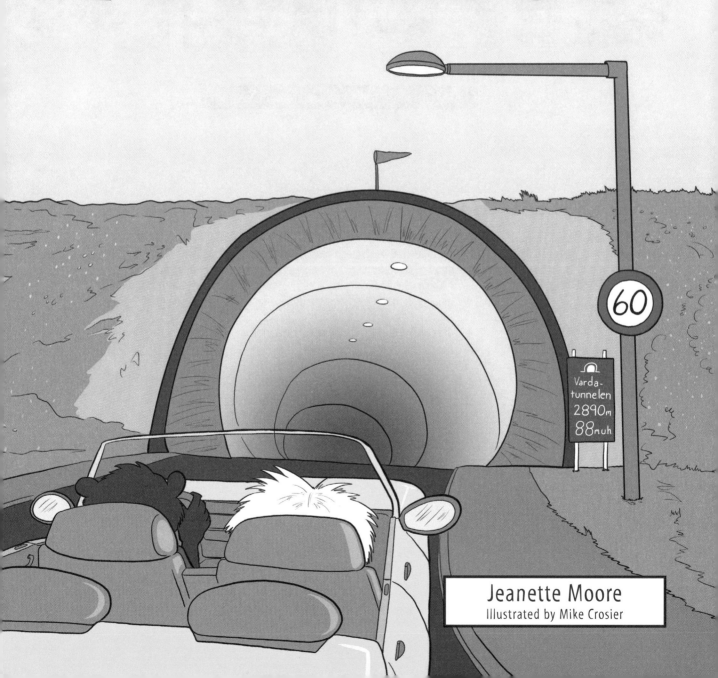

TUNNELS!

Vardatunnelen
2890m
88muh

60

Jeanette Moore
Illustrated by Mike Crosier

Titles in the **Explore Engineering** Set

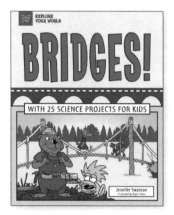
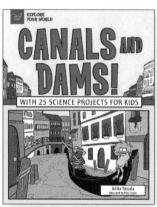

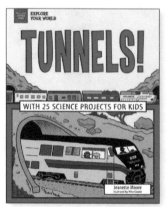

Check out more titles at www.nomadpress.net

Nomad Press
A division of Nomad Communications
10 9 8 7 6 5 4 3 2 1

This book was manufactured by Versa Press,
East Peoria, Illinois
August 2018, Job #J17-12598

ISBN Softcover: 978-1-61930-650-9
ISBN Hardcover: 978-1-61930-648-6

Educational Consultant, Marla Conn

Questions regarding the ordering of this book should be addressed to
Nomad Press
2456 Christian St.
White River Junction, VT 05001
www.nomadpress.net

Printed in the United States of America.

CONTENTS

Interested in primary sources? Look for this icon. Use a smartphone or tablet app to scan the QR code and explore more! Photos are also primary sources because a photograph takes a picture at the moment something happens.

If the QR code doesn't work, there's a list of URLs on the Resources page. Or, try searching the internet with the Keyword Prompts to find other helpful sources.

KEYWORD PROMPTS

tunnels

AROUND 47,000 BCE:
Neanderthal and early modern humans are the first human ancestors to tunnel as they expand the caves in which they live. Ancient remains about 49,000 years old are found in a deep, tunnel-like cave in Sidron, Spain, in 1994.

AROUND 9000 BCE:
Early modern humans leave murals on the walls of the caves and tunnels in southern France and northern Spain, where they hide during the end of the Ice Age.

AROUND 3000 BCE:
Babylonians build tunnels to transport water for irrigation.

AROUND 1000 BCE:
The Hohokam people of the Salt and Gila areas in what is now Phoenix, Arizona, build canals for irrigation.

680 BCE:
In the city of Gonabad, now part of Iran, a qanat provides drinking water and water for crops to almost 40,000 people! A qanat is a large underground tunnel that slopes downward and allows water to flow from inside a hill to wherever people need it.

1825–1842:
The waterway tunnel under the River Thames in London, England, is built using Brunel's shield, which makes tunneling safer for workers.

1666–1681 CE:
Gunpowder is used for the first time as a construction tool on the Canal du Midi. This canal was built across France and connected the Atlantic Ocean to the Mediterranean Sea.

1928:
The Posey Tunnel in California is the first highway tunnel built using the tube method, with circular shells made of steel and surrounded by concrete.

36 BCE:
Romans use the first hard-rock mining method, called fire-setting. They tunnel nearly 5,000 feet from Pozzuolo to Naples, Italy.

**2014–
THE FUTURE:**
The Kaneohe/Kailua Sewer Tunnel Project is a $173-million project for the city of Honolulu, Hawaii. The tunnel will be dug through basalt rock to move wastewater through large pipes.

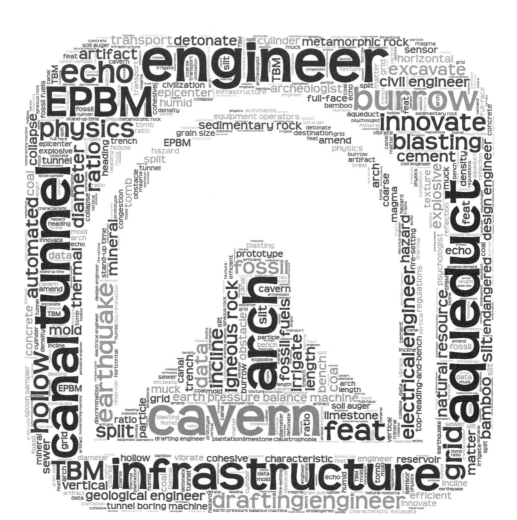

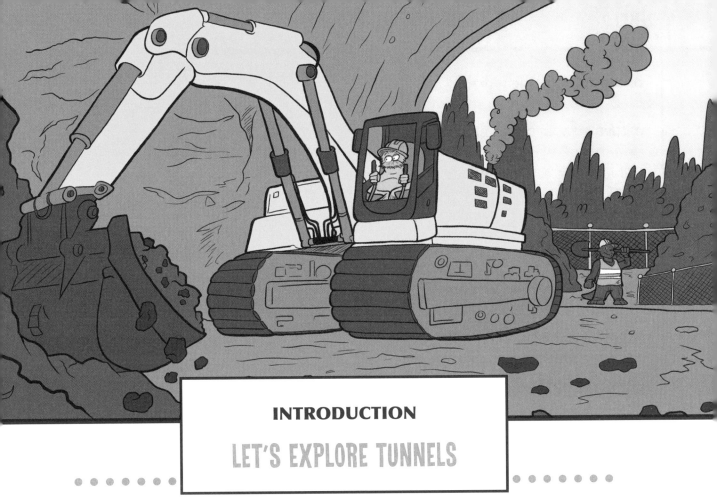

LET'S EXPLORE TUNNELS

Have you ever driven toward a city and the road goes underground? Maybe you've had to drive under a large body of water or through a mountain. Tunnels help drivers get to where they need to be. Without a tunnel, you'd have to go around the city, water, or mountain and add hours to your driving time!

Tunnels are hollow structures that exist underground. Some tunnels are dug by animals and insects. Many animals burrow in the dirt to go deep in the ground. They travel from place to place in their tunnels. Animals also store food, care for their young, and stay safe in tunnels.

WORDS TO KNOW

tunnel: a passageway that goes through or under natural or manmade obstacles, such as rivers, mountains, roads, and buildings.

hollow: having a hole or empty space inside.

burrow: to dig an underground hole or tunnel.

1

TUNNELS!

WORDS TO KNOW

obstacle: something that blocks your way.

natural resource: something from nature that people can use in some way, such as water, stone, and wood.

destination: the place to which someone or something is going.

arch: a curved structure in the shape of an upside-down U.

cylinder: a hollow tube shape.

WHAT IS A TUNNEL?

Humans dig tunnels for some of the same reasons as animals! People dig tunnels so they can move through or under **obstacles**, such as rivers and mountains. Tunnels can also move water from one place to another. Some tunnels are used to bring coal and other **natural resources** out of the ground.

A tunnel is a passageway to another space. Tunnels can take us to the other side of a mountain, deep underground, and even beneath the ocean. Tunnels allow us to move to new **destinations**.

The tunnels we use are usually manmade. That means a person or group of people designed and built the tunnel for a reason. Some tunnels are shaped like an **arch**, which looks like half of a **cylinder**, or tube. Other tunnels are round, like a complete cylinder.

A tunnel is hollow. There is space in it, and nothing else! Because a tunnel has sides and a roof, the wind from the outside can be blocked. Sometimes, though, wind can be created by vehicles passing through the tunnel.

Have you ever shouted while in a tunnel or a cave? What did it sound like? You might have heard an echo. An echo is a reflection of sound. The sound created by your voice travels down the tunnel and bounces off the walls, making a repeating sound. The echo extends sound right along the length of the tunnel.

Humans have been designing tunnels for thousands of years. Early humans used tunnels for shelter, just as animals do. Now, humans use tunnels to transport things. Tunnels serve as ways to get items from one place to another. We can travel through them with our cars, trucks, and trains. Even boats travel through tunnels!

WORDS ⊙ KNOW

echo: a sound caused by the reflection of sound waves from a surface back to the listener.

reflection: when light or sound hits an object and bounces off it.

length: the measurement of something from end to end.

transport: to move goods or people from one place to another.

DID YOU KNOW?

Do you have satellite radio in your car? Sometimes, a person driving through a tunnel will discover that their satellite radio stops working. This is because the satellite signal is blocked by the soil and rock around the tunnel, so the service is interrupted until they come out the other end. This can happen to cell phones, too.

irrigate: to supply land with water so that crops and plants will grow.

fossil fuels: coal, oil, and natural gas. These non-renewable energy sources come from the fossils of plants and tiny animals that lived millions of years ago.

sewer: a drain for wastewater.

cavern: a cave, especially one that is large and mostly underground.

earthquake: a sudden movement in pieces of the outer layer of the earth.

WORDS TO KNOW

DID YOU KNOW?

Early civilizations dug tunnels to irrigate, or water, their crops. Today, some gardeners still use tunnels to bring water to their plants.

Tunnels are also used to transport **fossil fuels,** such as natural gas, crude oil, and propane. These products provide us with energy for our homes. Tunnels are dug for plumbing, **sewers,** and to transport water. Powerlines can even be placed in underground tunnels, to bring electricity to large cities and local neighborhoods.

NATURAL TUNNELS

Humans make tunnels, animals make tunnels, and sometimes the earth itself makes tunnels! There are many natural tunnels found in countries all around the world. Natural tunnels can be formed by hollows, or **caverns,** that have been carved in the earth by water or other natural events, such as **earthquakes.**

Natural tunnels can be interesting and beautiful to explore. Because humans have no control over where they are formed, it's rare that we find natural tunnels useful.

fossil: the remains or traces of ancient plants or animals.

WORDS ⊚ KNOW

Gigantic pieces of the earth's crust are always moving. Sometimes, one layer goes under and another layer slides on top of it, creating connected caves and tunnels. In some of the walls of these tunnels, people have found fossils from ancient plant and animal life. Sometimes, natural tunnels get destroyed by earthquakes or other disasters!

In California, there is a natural cave called the Subway Cave in Lassen National Forest. Also called the "Old Lava Tube," the cave is one-third of a mile long. It is pitch black inside and usually only about 46 degrees Fahrenheit (8 degrees Celsius). It has the shape of half a cylinder.

WHAT DID ONE TUNNEL MAKER SAY TO THE OTHER TUNNEL MAKER?

HA HA HA

I dig you!

The Subway Cave has rough and jagged floors. These floors developed less than 20,000 years ago, when lava flowed from cracks in the earth. The lava poured and poured. Eventually, all this lava hardened into tube-like caves. Part of the roof of a cave collapsed and the entrance was formed.

TUNNEL TREES

Tunnels go through mountains and underground, but what about through a tree? In the nineteenth century, people created tunnels through redwoods as a way to attract visitors, not understanding that this could be damaging to the tree. One a few tunneled trees remain standing today.

TUNNELS!

Sometimes, people dig tunnels to connect natural caves. This is true in the country of Turkey, in the underground city of Derinkuyu. Here, there's a network of tunnels that served as a city long ago in the year 780. This area under the surface of the earth could hold 20,000 people! **Archaeologists** have discovered many **artifacts**, such as pottery, in these underground chambers.

THE TUNNEL OF LOVE

Some tunnels are manmade, but still surrounded by nature. How? Sometimes, the natural surroundings of an area work together in a tunnel structure. One example of this is the Tunnel of Love in the Ukraine. This is a long railway that trees have grown up and over to form a leafy green tunnel.

Legend has it that if a couple walks through the Tunnel of Love, they will stay together forever. Maybe that's why so many people have their wedding photos taken there!

(CREDIT: SERHEI)

TUNNEL WORK

Engineers are people who use science, math, and creativity to solve problems. People who design tunnels are often civil engineers. They figure out the design and materials that will work best for the purpose of the tunnel. A team of construction workers builds the tunnel based on the designs of the engineers.

Many of the workers on a tunnel job site are equipment operators. These men and women operate heavy machinery to get the job done. They might use big machines to excavate the ground and move pipes and concrete. They also use machines to dig trenches, start tunnels, and to smooth the walls of the tunnels.

Tunneling is known to be tough work. Many tunnel workers train on the job, quickly learning the dangers from their fellow workers.

engineer: a person who uses science, math, and creativity to design and build things.

civil engineer: someone who designs structures such as public roads, bridges, buildings, and tunnels.

equipment operator: someone who uses heavy equipment when working on a construction site.

excavate: to dig a hole or channel in the ground, or to make a hole by removing earth.

concrete: a construction material made with **cement**, sand, and water that hardens.

cement: lime powder and clay mixed with water that hardens and joins objects together.

trench: a ditch dug into the ground.

WORDS to KNOW

Many construction projects in New York City require underground excavating. People who do this are sometimes called "sandhogs." **Watch a video clip from a documentary on sandhogs at this website.**

KEYWORD PROMPTS

sandhogs greatest tunnel 🔍

hazard: a danger or risk.

infrastructure: roads, bridges, and other basic types of structures and equipment needed for a country to function properly.

WORDS TO KNOW

Tunnels are often in tight spaces. There might be very little air to breathe. Some tunnel workers bring in big fans and special blowers to get air into the area.

Tunnel workers also have to keep track of who is going in and out of the tunnel. It can be very dark underground and the workers don't always see each other! It is important for the person in charge of the project to take a head count so they know who is in the space.

Another serious **hazard** is fire. Fire can travel quickly in such a tight space. Water is another danger. Water can make tunnels slippery to work in.

Tunnels are a fascinating part of our **infrastructure**. Engineers are constantly working to find new ways of building stronger, safer tunnels. In this book, you'll discover the different uses of

tunnels, how different types of tunnels are used for different purposes, what's involved in building a tunnel, and some famous tunnels throughout history!

GOOD ENGINEERING PRACTICES

Engineers and scientists keep their ideas organized in notebooks. Engineers use the engineering design process to keep track of their inventions, and scientists use the scientific method to keep track of experiments. As you read through this book and do the activities, record your observations, **data**, and designs in an engineering design worksheet or a scientific method worksheet. When doing an activity, remember that there is no right answer or right way to approach a project. Be creative and have fun!

Engineering Design Worksheet
Problem: What problem are we trying to solve?
Research: Has anything been invented to help solve the problem? What can we learn?
Question: Are there any special requirements for the device? What is it supposed to do?
Brainstorm: Draw lots of designs for your device and list the materials you are using!
Prototype: Build the design you drew during brainstorming. This is your **prototype**.
Results: Test your prototype and record your observations.
Evaluate: Analyze your test results. Do you need to make adjustments? Do you need to try a different prototype?

Scientific Method Worksheet
Question: What problem are we trying to solve?
Research: What information is already known?
Hypothesis/Prediction: What do I think the answer will be?
Equipment: What supplies do I need?
Method: What steps will I follow?
Results: What happened and why?

A-MAZE-ING TUNNELS

The underground city of Derinkuyu in Turkey was made of a series of tunnels and caves, which could fit about 20,000 people! The city had stables, cellars, storage rooms, and chapels, just like an aboveground city. You can make your own tunnel city.

SUPPLIES

* engineering notebook and pencil
* toilet and paper towel tubes
* large cardboard box or plastic bin
* tape
* scissors
* ruler

1 Sketch designs for your tunnel city in your engineering notebook. This is your brainstorming step! Your city should fit into your box. What kinds of services do you need to provide for in your city? What will people eat? Where will they go to school? Where will they keep their animals? Decide how long and wide each of your tunnels and caves needs to be for its intended purpose.

2 Make your prototype. Cut the tubes to the right lengths. Begin to lay out the tubes according to your design. Is there anything you need to change? What material can you use for caves?

ESSENTIAL QUESTIONS

Each chapter of this book begins with an essential question to help guide your exploration of tunnels. Keep the question in your mind as you read the chapter. At the end of each chapter, use your engineering notebook to record your thoughts and answers.

INVESTIGATE!

Why are tunnels useful in big cities where there are lots of people?

THE UNDERGROUND CITY OF DERINKUYU

(CREDIT: HELEN COOK)

3 Evaluate your design and change anything you think could be better. Is there anything you'd like to add?

4 When you are satisfied with your city, tape the tunnels into the box to keep them in place. Are you able to make a continuous tunnel all the way around your city?

TRY THIS! Design a second level for your tunnel city. How will your city dwellers get from one level to another? Do you need to add stairs or ladders? How will food and water be transported through your multi-level city?

CHAPTER 1

WHY DO WE BUILD TUNNELS?

Imagine if there were no tunnels in the United States. What might our roads be like? What would our cities look like? How would energy get to your home? Tunnels serve many purposes to make our lives better.

Humans need tunnels for several different reasons. We use tunnels to transport people, waste, water, and even energy. More than 400 tunnels in the United States were built for one of these purposes. Do you know of a tunnel near you? What is its purpose? Let's take a look at some of the ways tunnels solve problems.

 INVESTIGATE!

What are some of the reasons people need tunnels?

TUNNELS FOR TRANSPORTATION

The first tunnels used for transportation were **canal** tunnels. For example, the Bridgewater Canal Tunnel in England was built in 1761 to carry **coal** from mines to the city of Manchester.

When trains were introduced in the 1800s, many more tunnels were needed for the trains to pass through. Tunnels allow trains to travel through mountains and hills. What would a train trip be like if there were no tunnels along the way? There would be a lot of ups and downs! By going through tunnels, trains can avoid steep **inclines** that can be dangerous, especially in bad weather.

People traveling by car can also benefit from tunnels, which help keep cities from becoming too **congested** with traffic. Have you ever been stuck in traffic on your way someplace? You might know what it's like to spend hours in a car, able to move very little because of all the other cars around yours.

canal: a manmade waterway built for shipping, navigation, or irrigation.

coal: a dark brown or black rock formed from decayed plants. Coal is a fossil fuel.

incline: a slope, especially on a road or railway.

congestion: when something is filled to excess, crowded, or overburdened.

WORDS TO KNOW

DID YOU KNOW?

The Gotthard Base Tunnel, completed in 2016, is the longest and deepest train tunnel in the world. It travels 35 miles through the Alps in Switzerland, taking passengers up to 1.4 miles underground!

Tunnels make it possible for cars to travel on several different levels, so everyone can get to where they're going faster.

In some places around the world, tunnels help people travel from island to island. One of these tunnels is the Seikan Tunnel in Japan, which took 17 years to complete!

The Seikan Tunnel was built under the sea and connects the island of Honshu to another island named Hokkaido. The trains can only go 7 miles per hour through this tunnel or else the trains produce too powerful an air current. If the current gets too strong, it can push a passing train off the tracks. Engineers are currently working to improve this underwater passageway.

DID YOU KNOW?

The world's car traffic continues to increase every year. Underground tunnels can make new routes for travelers to help them to get from point A to point B.

WHO INVENTED UNDERGROUND TUNNELS?

HA HA HA

A mole!

SEWER TUNNELS

Tunnels have been used for sewers for thousands of years. Today, sewer systems are a regular part of every city and town. Contaminated water can cause disease to spread, so people have thought up **innovative** ways to move this water away from where people live.

BCE: put after a date, BCE stands for Before Common Era and counts down to zero. CE stands for Common Era and counts up from zero. This book was printed in 2018 CE.

WORDS ᴛᴏ KNOW

You can still find sewer tunnels that were constructed hundreds of years ago. The ancient stone tunnels that run underneath the Italian city of Rome are made of strong rock. The most well-known of these tunnels is the Cloaca Maxima, or the "Giant Sewer." This tunnel travels under the Roman Forum, which used to be a place where ancient Romans sold livestock.

The Cloaca Maxima empties into the Tiber River. It's about 1 mile long and was built around 600 BCE at the order of the last king of Rome, Tarquin the Proud (died 495 BCE). Today, a small trickle of water still flows through the Giant Sewer!

A DRAWING OF THE GIANT SEWER IN ROME FROM 1842
(CREDIT: JEREMIAH DONOVAN, BRITISH LIBRARY)

HEZEKIAH'S TUNNEL

Hezekiah's Tunnel was built in 700 BCE in Jerusalem, Israel. It is even mentioned in the Bible! King Hezekiah (739 BCE–687 BCE) ordered the 1,740-foot-long tunnel to be constructed so the city's water could be protected from attackers.

A SECTION OF HEZEKIAH'S TUNNEL
(CREDIT: TAMAR HAYARDENI)

Ancient Rome was well known for its sewage systems. Many public baths and bathrooms had plumbing, which helped keep areas clean and free of germs.

Even before the ancient Romans, the Babylonians were known for constructing sewage systems between 5000 BCE and 539 BCE. Pipes made out of copper and lead were placed in tunnels to remove waste from the cities.

Tunnels have always been an important part of sewers, both ancient and new.

MOVING WATER

We've seen how tunnels help with transportation and waste removal. They are also great for moving water from one place to another. This is useful for draining water from a town, moving water away from a home, or watering crops that grow far from a water source.

The earliest **aqueducts** date back to the Minoans on what is now the Greek island of Crete. Around 2000 BCE, the Minoans used tiles and pipes to channel water from one place to another in simple tunnels.

Other cultures, including those in ancient Persia, Egypt, and China, built more complex systems of aqueducts. These systems sometimes included **reservoirs**, where water could collect before being sent through tunnels to wherever it was needed.

In Rome, some of the ancient aqueducts sent water to fountains and gardens. Rome is known for its many beautiful fountains! Many tunnels provided water for growing crops.

The aqueducts of the Catskill Mountains in upstate New York transport water from two reservoirs. The reservoirs hold water that is good for drinking and using in your sink or bathtub.

BUILDING THE CATSKILL AQUEDUCT
(CREDIT: CASSIER'S MAGAZINE, 1891)

The water from these reservoirs is pumped to New York City! In fact, the Catskill Aqueduct provides New York City with 40 percent of its water.

Today, giant tunnels in Tokyo protect this Japanese city from overflowing with water. Japan's capital of 13 million people is in a high-risk area for flooding and tropical storms, so some safety measures had to be put in place! Tunnels help drain water from heavy rainfalls away from the most populated areas of the city so they aren't flooded.

DID YOU KNOW?

The Delaware Aqueduct in New York is the longest tunnel in the whole world. It is 85 miles long and is New York City's main water supply.

TUNNELS OF DIRT

Traffic, waste, water—what else travels through tunnels?

Even before people used tunnels to transport water, they used tunnels to transport stones, metals, coal, and other materials that people use. Have you ever seen a diamond ring? That diamond was mined—it was dug out of the ground and probably carried through a tunnel to the surface.

Ancient people dug for materials, such as a rock called flint, to make weapons and tools. Ancient Egyptians mined the earth for a mineral called malachite. This green stone was used to decorate pottery.

The Egyptians also mined gold for jewelry and other precious items. We can still see the artifacts of their civilization in museums today! Many of these precious metals and gems were transported through tunnels.

Humans also dig for oil under the earth! The first American oil tunnels were dug in Sulphur Mountain in California in the 1860s. These were dug by hand. The crude oil from the tunnels was taken away by horse-drawn wagons. Then the oil was transported to San Francisco, California.

PERSEVERE!

The Guoliang Tunnel is in the Tailhang Mountains of China. It is considered one of the world's most dangerous roadways and is one of the only ways to get to Hunan Province. It was created by 13 villagers who hand-dug the tunnel and even lined it with windows. Construction of the tunnel took five years! The tunnel is three-quarters of a mile long, 16 feet tall, and 13 feet wide.

You can watch cars and people travel through the Guoliang Tunnel at this website.

KEYWORD PROMPTS

Guoliang Tunnel video

TUNNELS!

Oil companies such as the Union Oil Co. worked to make the tunnels better and safer for the miners. The engineers developed a system of mirrors to reflect sunlight into the tunnels, so workers could better see what they were doing. This lighting system was based on a method used by ancient Egyptians when they tunneled into the earth to build **tombs**!

ENERGY UNDERGROUND

Power tunnels are filled with wires and underground electrical systems that bring electricity to cities and towns. In 2011, in London, England, the National Grid system started a project digging some of these deep underground power tunnels.

THIS TUNNEL HOLDS PIPES THAT CARRY STEAM IN COPENHAGEN, DENMARK.
(CREDIT: BILL EBBESEN)

These tunnels give London access to energy. The tunnels are far below the roads and carry high-voltage electrical cables that distribute electricity to many areas.

Underground power line tunnels are also found in Stockholm, Sweden. These tunnels replace the power lines that are found on poles. Do you have wires and poles in your neighborhood? In Stockholm, the wires lie safely underground in rock tunnels.

Now that we know some of the ways tunnels are used around the world, in the next chapter we'll look at the engineering and design that go into making sure these tunnels are safe!

CONSIDER AND DISCUSS

It's time to consider and discuss: What are some of the reasons people need tunnels?

ENERGY INFRASTRUCTURE

Many companies and governments around the world have programs that maintain roads, tunnels, pipelines, bridges, and canals. This infrastructure has to do with transportation. There is also infrastructure that has to do with getting energy from its source to its destination, such as your house! Why do the lights come on when you flick the switch? Because the energy infrastructure has been maintained. Energy infrastructure includes oil refineries, power lines, and gas tanks.

PROJECT!

GRID PLANNING

SUPPLIES

✳ grid paper (or draw your own)

✳ ruler

✳ markers or colored pencils

✳ engineering notebook and pencil

When they plan underground power line tunnels, and many other types of tunnels, engineers use a grid to design the layout of the tunnels. Try designing your own tunnels using a grid.

1 Use a ruler to draw a grid like the one shown here in your notebook or, with an adult's permission, print grid paper (also called graph paper) from this website.

2 Decide what kind of tunnels you want to design and label your grid with that name. Are you going to design a power line, a train tunnel, or an aqueduct?

PROJECT!

3 Label the vertical part of the grid with numbers, starting with 1 at the very bottom left corner, and then moving up to 2, 3, 4, and so on. Label the horizontal part of the grid with letters. The line to the right of the first row is A, followed by B and C and so on. This is what the horizontal bottom portion of the grid should look like:

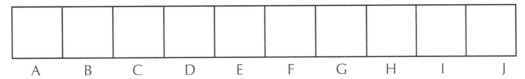

A   B   C   D   E   F   G   H   I   J

4 Use a pencil to draw tunnels on your grid. Do you need to make sure the tunnels don't cross? Do you need them to cross at certain points? Why? You can erase tunnels if you make a wrong turn!

5 Write in your notebook where the bends are in your tunnels. For example, you can make a list:

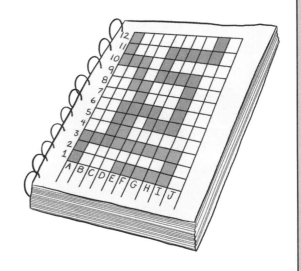

- Left Bend 1 is located at D3

- Right Bend 1 is located at E5

- Left Bend 2 is located at A5

6 Once you complete your plan, go over your pencil lines with markers or colored pencils.

TRY THIS! Make a larger grid. Go all the way to the end of the alphabet on a large piece of graph paper. What kind of project might need such a large tunnel system? What is different about designing a larger system?

SUPPLIES

* square of cardboard
* lump of clay the size of your fist
* tools to push through the clay (small spoons, pens)
* Popsicle sticks
* five 4-inch long pipe cleaners
* water

BE A TUNNEL ENGINEER

With more and more cars and trucks on the road every year, the world's engineers are constructing new tunnels every day. Sometimes, they have to go through mountains in order to create a tunnel for trains and cars to pass through. Let's explore how we can make a model of this process!

1 Take the cardboard square and put your name on it. This is your work station!

2 Place the lump of clay onto your work station. Begin to mold it into the shape of a cylinder. Roll it if you need to get more of a cylinder shape. Use your tools to make a hole through the cylinder of clay.

3 Place Popsicle sticks around the entrance and exit of the tunnel. Run pipe cleaners along the middle of the tunnel to give it structure.

4 Smooth the outside of the clay with a small amount of water.

5 Give your tunnel a name!

THINK ABOUT IT: Research a famous tunnel constructor. Head to the library or ask an adult if you can use a computer to read about how this person learned to build tunnels and what makes their tunnels famous.

CHAPTER 2

ENGINEERS AND DESIGNS

Have you ever seen workers building a tunnel? They use lots of big machines and many different plans to make the process go smoothly. It's very important that the tunnels are designed and built according to careful plans so that no one gets hurt either during the building process or when using the tunnels after they're completed!

No one wants a tunnel to **collapse**! Many types of engineers use different methods of designing and building tunnels so the whole project is successful.

These people must understand **physics** to design and build tunnels.

WORDS TO KNOW

collapse: to fall in or down suddenly.

physics: the science of how matter and energy work together.

25

matter: what an object is made of.

force: a push or a pull that causes a change of motion in an object.

shear: a sliding force that slips parts of a material in opposite directions.

compression: a pushing force that squeezes or presses material inward.

tension: a pulling force that pulls or stretches an object.

torsion: a twisting force.

WORDS TO KNOW

? INVESTIGATE!

Why are there different methods of building different tunnels?

Physics is the study of **matter** and how it behaves when **forces** act on it. Tunnel engineers pay special attention to four different forces when designing a tunnel—**shear, compression, tension,** and **torsion.**

Let's take a look at the different forces that can act on a tunnel.

SHEARING FORCE

A shearing force happens when parts of the tunnel are pushed in different directions. Can you think of an event when this would happen?

How about an earthquake? During an earthquake, dirt, rock, and soil are moved up and down or back and forth.

Parts of the ground that are side by side scrape against each other because of the shearing force caused by an earthquake. Tunnels must be built with strong materials to withstand shearing force.

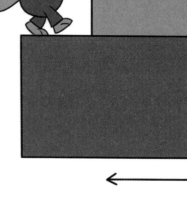

COMPRESSION FORCE

Compression happens when the materials that form a tunnel are squeezed together. Imagine pushing down on a slinky—what happens? Now imagine that same force pushing down on a tunnel. But, instead of bouncing back up like a slinky, a tunnel that's been compressed from the top down will need lots of repairs!

In a tunnel, compression occurs when the weight above is too heavy for the materials that support it. If the force of compression is too strong, materials can buckle or snap.

TENSION FORCE

Tension and compression work together when a tunnel is pressed down from above. While compression pushes materials together, tension pulls materials apart.

What happens when you place a heavy object on a marshmallow? While parts of the marshmallow will be compressed, other parts experience tension and spread apart. The base of the marshmallow will spread apart because of the weight above it.

TORSION FORCE

Torsion is another word for "twisting." This occurs when opposite forces are applied to an object on different sides. For example, if you hold a plastic ruler in your hands and twist both ends of it in opposite directions, what happens? Cracks will begin to form on the ruler as parts of it are pulled away from other parts. Now, imagine this happening in a tunnel!

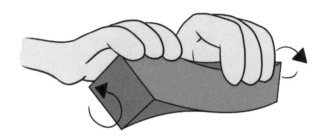

You might have noticed that many tunnels are round tubes. That's because with a tube shape, pressure from the outside is most evenly distributed. With a square or rectangle, there tends to be more pressure in certain places. If a tunnel is shaped as a square or rectangle, it is more likely to collapse.

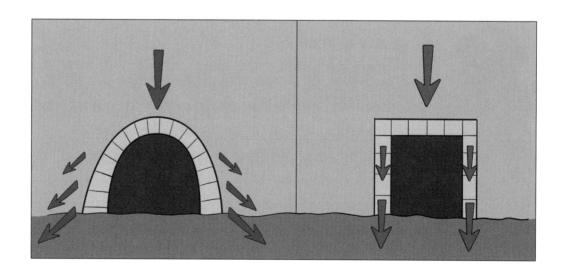

ENGINEERS ON A TUNNEL JOB

Civil engineers specialize in building bridges and tunnels. They work with the construction team and direct the project so they can make these structures safe.

What if there is a hurricane? Could the tunnel handle lots of water? These are questions civil engineers work to answer. They need to know what kinds of material the tunnel will be dug through, where the tunnel needs to go, and what regulations need to be followed in the designing of the tunnel.

All towns and states have building regulations for structures such as tunnels, bridges, and buildings. These regulations keep the structures, and the people who use them, safe!

Drafting engineers create the finished plans. They present all the ideas on paper and on a computer, so the builders will know what steps need to be taken and when. Also called design engineers, they take many measurements to create models and other prototypes.

Geotechnical engineers are involved in mining, forestry, and geography. They understand the soil, the location of rocks, and the places where there is water.

Is the area too wet or too dry for certain materials or equipment to be used in the tunnel? Geotechnical engineers will know! They want to make sure the tunnel is placed properly in the ground or in the water to ensure everyone's safety.

This engineer might also locate fossil fuels or mineral deposits in the area that are to be dug up for a tunnel. Sometimes, natural resources such as oil, gas, tar sands, and even coal are found underground. A geological engineer surveys the land and makes sure the area is perfect for building.

Electrical engineers understand the lighting and wiring that is required at the building site. They make a plan to install the wiring needed to provide power to the tunnels that need it, such as a subway tunnel.

DESIGN TECHNIQUES

Would you build a tunnel through sand the same way you'd build a tunnel through rock? Different techniques are used to build different types of tunnels for the best outcomes. Let's look at some examples.

Full-face and top-heading-and-bench are two basic ways tunnels are engineered and designed. Before deciding which technique to use, engineers first look at the type of ground they'll be digging in. Soft ground, which includes silt, sand, gravel, dirt, and mud, is easy to dig through. Not surprisingly, it is difficult to dig through hard rock.

When engineers decide to use a full-face technique, they work on the entire diameter of the tunnel at the same time. Think of the opening of a tunnel—it's in the shape of a circle. The distance across that circle is the diameter of the tunnel.

diameter

WORDS TO KNOW

full-face: a method of constructing tunnels that involves digging the entire diameter of the tunnel at the same time.

top-heading-and-bench: a method of constructing tunnels that involves digging layers of the tunnel from the top down.

silt: soil made up of fine bits of rock.

diameter: the distance across a circle through the middle.

automated: controlled by a computer instead of by a person.

sensor: a device that takes measurements and gives a computer information about its surroundings.

SELF-DRIVING SUBWAY

Subway systems are built with tunnels. New York City subways might soon have **automated** cars that drive themselves! These cars will have **sensors** all around them to know if something is in the way of the subway car, and computer systems will control the navigation. A two-way communication system will let passengers talk to people in control booths. What are some of the good things about automated subway systems? Are there any bad things?

heading: in top-heading-and-bench construction, a small tunnel that is the start of a larger tunnel.

bench: in top-heading-and-bench construction, the area that is excavated below the heading.

WORDS ⊕ KNOW

DID YOU KNOW?

Tunnels have been built for the safety of animals, not just humans! More than 600 tunnels have been dug under roads in the Netherlands to help endangered animals such as the European badger cross dangerous roadways.

Engineers use a full-face technique for smaller tunnels. It's also best for tunnels that are going through hard ground.

The top-heading-and-bench technique is different. Workers dig a mini tunnel first, above the area where the tunnel is planned. This is called a **heading**. Once the heading is in place, workers excavate the area just below the floor of the heading in a process called top-heading.

The excavated area is called a **bench**. Workers dig more benches below the first one until the entire area is excavated. This top-heading-and-bench process helps tunnel engineers know if the rock below is stable.

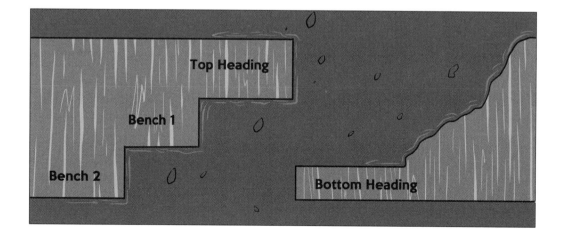

If the heading remains strong, they can continue digging benches without fear of a cave-in. The top-heading-and-bench technique is a good method for building a tunnel in soft soil.

BLAST OFF!

Tunneling through tough, hard rock can be tricky! Engineers sometimes use **blasting** to break up the rock.

Blasting is just like what it sounds. Holes are drilled in the rock around a tunnel's face, either by hand or by a large machine called a drilling jumbo, and those holes are packed with **explosives**. These explosives are then **detonated**.

blasting: removing rocks and materials with the use of explosives.

explosive: a substance that is used to blow up structures.

detonate: to explode or cause to explode.

fire-setting: the process of using fire and water to soften and crack rock.

WORDS ⏀ KNOW

HOT AND COLD

Before explosives were invented and used in mining, workers used a process called **fire-setting** to break down rock. A tunnel wall was heated with fire and then cooled with water. This heating and cooling caused the wall to expand and contract, which weakened it so that chunks fell off. Ancient Romans used this technique to build the Cloaca Maxima sewer you learned about in Chapter 1.

muck: material removed during the process of excavating.

metamorphic rock: rock that has been transformed by heat or pressure or both into new rock, while staying solid.

igneous rock: rock that forms from cooling magma.

magma: hot, melted rock below the surface of the earth.

sedimentary rock: rock formed from the compression of sediments, the remains of plants and animals, or the evaporation of seawater.

limestone: a sedimentary rock that forms from the skeletons and shells of sea creatures.

WORDS ⊙ KNOW

After the fumes are vacuumed out, the workers remove the rubble and debris, called **muck,** so they can continue digging the tunnel. This process is often repeated.

Tunnel engineers work together to create some of the most interesting and useful tunnels in the world. In Chapter 4, we'll look at some of the different types of tunnels these engineers design.

CONSIDER AND DISCUSS

It's time to consider and discuss: Why are there different methods of building different tunnels?

TYPES OF ROCK

Workers and engineers can find three kinds of rock when they are tunneling. **Metamorphic rocks** form under the earth because of super-high heat and pressure. Marble is an example of metaphoric rock. **Igneous rock** is formed when **magma** cools deep in the earth. Basalt and granite are types of igneous rock. What smaller word can you find in "sedimentary?" **Sedimentary rocks** are made from sediment, or tiny pieces of minerals, bits of plants, and even fossils. **Limestone** and chalk are examples of sedimentary rock.

MOVING MATERIALS

Before machinery was available, workers used carts to bring the muck out of the tunnels after they were blasted. Hauling away material was nothing new for these workers, but it was heavy work! Let's find out which materials weigh the most.

SUPPLIES

* materials from outside (sand, gravel, pebbles, rocks, dirt)
* 5 paper or plastic cups
* scale
* engineering notebook and pencil

1 Gather different types of material from outdoors. You may be in your yard or behind the school. Look for sand, gravel, pebbles, rocks, and dirt. Keep each kind of material separate.

2 Place the same amount of material into each cup. The five cups for the five materials should be the same size. You may fill them all halfway, or all the way. It depends on how much material you have collected!

3 Draw a chart like this in your notebook. Place each cup on the scale. Record the weight in your notebook with your pencil.

Materials	Weight in ounces	Weight in grams
sand		
gravel		
pebbles		
rocks		
dirt		

4 Which one weighed the most? Even though there was a similar amount of material in each cup, certain types of materials are heavier than others. These are harder to move without machinery to help!

TRY THIS! Find more materials to weigh. Can you find any wood chips? Different types of rock? Small pieces of brick or cement? Go on a materials hunt and add the information to your chart.

TOILET PAPER ENGINEERING

Do you use toilet paper? Sure! Look at the cardboard tubes in the toilet paper rolls. These are tiny tunnels! The center of a paper towel roll also contains a cardboard tunnel. Let's build some cardboard tunnels!

SUPPLIES

* ruler
* paper towel tubes
* toilet paper tubes
* duct tape or electrical tape
* a wall where it is okay to tape a tube (brick or cement wall is best)
* aluminum foil
* a bin
* engineering notebook and pencil

1 Start an engineering design worksheet and think about how long you want your tunnel to be. Take a few measurements. How long is your shortest tube? How long is your longest tube? Write down the measurements in your notebook.

2 Sketch your design. How many rolls will you need for your tunnel? Begin connecting your tube pieces with tape.

3 Find a spot to tape your tunnel. It should be a concrete, cement, or brick wall, so no marks are left from the tape. Do not use a wall that is painted! As you tape your tunnel, aim it slightly downward to give it a slope.

4 Roll small balls of foil that can fit in the tunnel and roll through. Place a bin on the ground below the exit point of your tunnel. Aim your tinfoil balls down the sloping tunnel into the bin!

5 Change the slope of the tunnel. What happens when it is more slanted? Less slanted? Do the balls move faster or slower? Record your findings in your engineering notebook.

TRY THIS! Before hanging your tunnel, grab some of your favorite paints. Acrylics are great to work with and easy to wash. Decorate the tunnel, or tunnels, with fun designs. Maybe they could look like cave art! Or find some pictures of hieroglyphics to place on your tunnels.

MATH IN SCIENCES

The diameters of the entry point and exit point of the tunnel is important. When engineers decide how wide a tunnel will be, they consider many factors. What will go through the tunnel? Is it wide enough for cars? People? The diameter is the length from the left to the right of the tunnel. It is a straight line across the tunnel entrance (or exit) that is important to the planning of any tunnel.

1 Take a piece of paper and roll it into a narrow cylinder. Place your eye at the end of this cylinder-shaped paper. Tube 1 should be like a telescope.

2 Use two or three small pieces of Scotch tape to secure the tube in place.

3 Use the ruler to measure the diameter across one end of the tube. It should be the same on the other end. Write down this measurement in your notebook.

4 Take another piece of paper and roll it so it has the diameter of a can of soup. Tube 2 should be larger than Tube 1. Tape the paper.

5 Use the ruler to measure the diameter across one end of the tube. It should be the same on the other end. Write down this measurement in your notebook. The diameter of Tube 2 should be larger than the diameter of Tube 1.

6 Take a third piece of paper and roll it to an even larger diameter. It may even fit on your head! Tape the tube.

7 Use the ruler to measure the diameter across one end of the tube. It should be the same on the other end. Write down this measurement in your notebook. The diameter of Tube 3 should be larger than the diameters of both Tubes 1 and 2.

TRY THIS! Find objects in your home or school environment that have diameters. Maybe you'll find some round containers or mugs. What else can you find? You may be surprised by how many objects have diameters! Make a list of these objects. Measure their diameters. Put them in order, from smallest to largest.

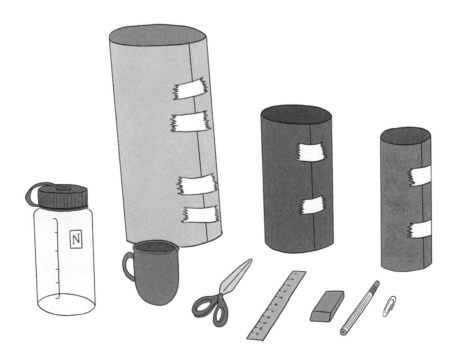

IT'S SEDIMENTARY

Sedimentary rock is made up of many kinds of rock. It can also contain shells, pebbles, and other small pieces of materials. Can you find sedimentary rocks where you live?

1 Locate a good spot for rock hunting. You are looking for sedimentary rocks, which are made of various materials.

2 Draw a sketch of the area you will be exploring. What are the surroundings like? For example, if you are at the seashore, you may think your sedimentary rock finds will contain shells.

3 Start a scientific method worksheet and make a hypothesis. What kinds of materials will the rocks in your area have? Record your answer in your engineering notebook.

4 Start looking! Pick up small rocks and analyze them with your magnifying glass.

5 Create a chart like the one on the next page and write down your findings. Draw detailed pictures.

6 Was your hypothesis true? Write a statement that explains what you found in the area you explored.

WHERE DO GEOLOGISTS LIKE TO RELAX?

HA HA HA

In a rocking chair!

PROJECT!

Sedimentary sample	Picture	I think it contains…
1		
2		
3		
4		

TRY THIS! Continue the hunt for rocks, but do this in another spot. In a separate chart, note your findings. Then compare your two locations. What was the difference between the two?

THAT'S SWELL

SUPPLIES

* plastic bottle with a cap
* small container of hot tap water (ask an adult to help with this)
* clock or timer
* partner
* small container of ice-cold water

Fire-setting makes rocks expand, or get bigger, and contract, or shrink. This process forces a rock to break. As chunks fall off, workers can slowly move into a hard, rocky area so they can build a tunnel. This expansion and contraction is thermal. **That means it relates to temperature. Changes in temperature can break rocks. Now that is powerful!**

1 Take the cap off the plastic bottle but keep it close by. Hold the bottle in the hot water for 2 to 3 minutes.

2 While the bottle is in the hot water, ask your partner to place the cap on the bottle. It should be screwed on tightly.

3 What happens to the bottle? **Particles** in the plastic bottle spread out when heated up.

4 Repeat steps 1 to 3 with the ice-cold water.

5 What happens to the bottle? Particles in the plastic bottle contract when cooled.

TRY THIS! Engineers use expansion joints to prevent tunnels from moving once the pieces of the tunnel have been built. Bridges also need expansion joints. Research expansion joints. Draw a diagram of a tunnel or bridge with an expansion joint.

WORDS to KNOW

thermal: related to heat.

particle: a tiny piece of matter.

PROJECT!

BERNOULLI WHO?

Daniel Bernouilli (1700–1782) discovered a principle that explains the relationship between air pressure **and tunnels. If the speed of a moving liquid or gas increases, then the pressure inside a tunnel decreases. This is true for pipes and small tunnels, too. Let's try this principle.**

SUPPLIES

* ❋ 2 plastic straws
* ❋ cup filled with water
* ❋ scissors
* ❋ engineering notebook and pencil

1 Place one of the straws in the cup of water. Cut the second straw in half to use as a blower.

2 Start a scientific method worksheet and make a prediction. What will happen if you blow across the top of the straw in the water? Write your hypothesis in your engineering notebook.

3 Use your short straw to blow across the top of the straw in the water. What happens to the water in the straw?

4 Why does this happen? When the air blows across the top of the straw, the air pressure at the spot is reduced. The pressure in the straw expands upward to fill in that space, and carries the water with it!

TRY THIS! Experiment with different straw lengths as your blower. How does the length of the blower affect what happens to the water? Record your results.

WORDS ⏀ KNOW

air pressure: the weight of air that is pressing down on the earth.

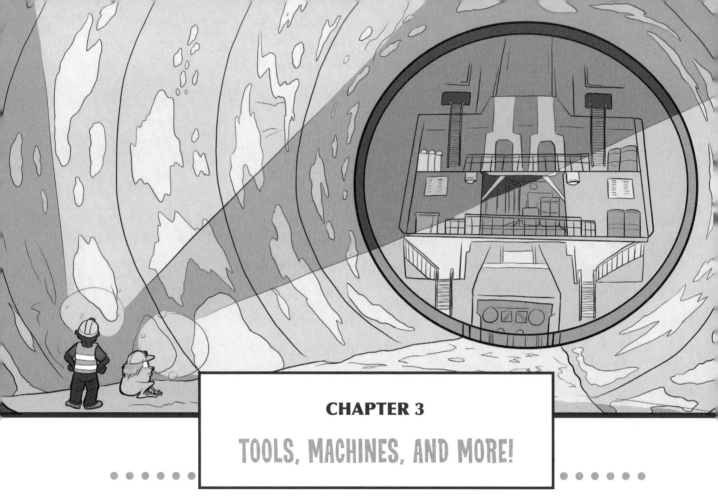

CHAPTER 3

TOOLS, MACHINES, AND MORE!

Tunnel construction involves lots of heavy equipment and machinery. After all, boulders and large rocks must be removed or blasted. Gigantic amounts of soil, silt, clay, and sand must be hauled away. Water must be blocked or moved toward a different location to make room for the tunnel construction.

The very first machine that starts a tunnel project is the human brain. People imagine what the tunnel needs to look like and where it can be placed. One of the first things engineers think about is the material where the tunnel will be dug. Geologists and engineers gather data about the dig site. They report on the land and its characteristics.

WORDS TO KNOW

geologist: a scientist who studies geology, which is the history and structure of Earth and its rocks.

characteristic: a feature of a person, place, or thing.

? INVESTIGATE!

What kind of machinery might people invent in the future to do the work of digging tunnels?

For example, the rock and materials that are on the surface of the land give clues as to what is under the ground. But the engineers must also investigate what is under the ground. This gives them information about the materials they will be able to use to construct the tunnel.

SOIL SAMPLING

Part of the geologic report tells builders what kind of soil lies beneath the surface. The U.S. Department of Agriculture has categories for different types of soil. There are 12 types of soil, called **textures**. The different textures are based on the **ratio** of sand, silt, and clay.

Geologists use a **soil auger** that digs into the ground and collects a sample of the ground to be tested. What is the ground made of? Engineers need to know this to plan tunnels.

WORDS TO KNOW

cohesive: holding together firmly or stickily.

sieve: a tool that is used for separating coarse material from fine material.

grain size: the size of clay, silt, or sand particles.

DID YOU KNOW?

The Komatsu D575A is the world's largest bulldozer and has even been called a "Super Dozer." It has a big front blade that can move enough material to fill three school buses.

Clay is the most **cohesive** soil. That means it sticks together best. Sand does not have as much cohesion as clay. Think of scooping up a handful of sand at the beach. Open your palm, and the sand slides out between your fingers and back to the ground. That is not cohesive!

Geologists also measure the size of the grains as they figure out which category the soil falls in. A device called a **sieve** measures the **grain size** by allowing smaller grains to fall through it first while the larger ones remain.

Most of the particles in soil are from sedimentary rocks. Sedimentary rocks are made of different kinds of matter, such as sand and shells and dirt. The grain size of each kind of material is different.

For example, fine sand has much smaller particles than **coarse** sand. This is information engineers need to know about a building site before they start digging.

When the geologists and people involved in the project know the type of soil they are going to be working with, they can better understand the strength of the soil. This includes the soil's **stand-up time**.

Stand-up time is the amount of time that goes by before unsupported sections of a tunnel begin to fall. Ground that has low stand-up time has lots of sand and gravel. That is because these materials aren't as cohesive as clay. Clay sticks together and is great for constructing tunnels.

DIVE!

Do you like sitting in your car during a traffic jam? Probably not! Inventor Elon Musk doesn't like it either. That's why he and his company are working on projects to create tunnel networks underneath big cities such as Los Angeles, California. Cars and vans will be able to enter these tunnels at street level and be lowered to an underground road to join the rest of the traffic zipping along to its destination. Sound good?

PS **You can read more about Elon Musk's ideas in this article.**

KEYWORD PROMPTS

Elon Musk Verge tunnel 🔍

Another tool a geologist uses is the **split-spoon sampler.** This measures the **density** of soil. A 140-pound hammer drives the sampler into the ground. The more times the split-spoon must be hit with the hammer to push it into the soil, the denser the soil.

LET'S GET EXCAVATING

Once the reports are complete and the ground passes inspection, then it is time to dig! In ancient times, shovels were the main tool, and workers dug by hand. But today, most of the digging is done with machinery.

The machine used most often when digging tunnels is a **tunnel boring machine (TBM).** It's a huge drill that can be used in almost any kind of material.

TBMs are cost-**efficient**, meaning they do lots of work for less money. They are very large machines that can be hard to transport to dig sites! There are also micro TBMs that do the same work on a smaller scale.

THE FRONT OF A TBM

TBMs have a rotating cutting wheel on the front that spins and cuts into the soil as it moves forward. Often, excavation leaves materials that need to be moved to another place. Bulldozers push and plow dirt and rocks out of the way, so the dump trucks can carry off the mess!

> **earth pressure balance machine (EPBM):** a large machine that bores through soft ground and uses the excavated material to support the tunnel walls.
>
> **WORDS ⯈ KNOW**

Construction projects require a team effort from engineers, geologists, planners, and workers alike. But the machines involved in tunnel making are also part of the team!

The next step in the construction of a tunnel is to build the lining. This is when material is placed to keep the tunnel from caving in. The lining is what you see instead of dirt when you drive through a tunnel!

EARTH PRESSURE BALANCE MACHINE

A certain kind of TBM—called an **earth pressure balance machine (EPBM)**—is designed to use the material it cuts from the front to create a substance that can be used to add support to the tunnel walls behind the machine. EPBMs are used in soft ground. This means the pressure from surrounding ground is less likely to cause a cave-in, because the new material supports the tunnel walls right away.

beam: a rigid, horizontal structure that carries a load.

WORDS ⓣⓞ KNOW

LINING THE TUNNEL

Many years ago, construction workers used brick and cast iron for the lining of tunnels. Now, concrete and steel are used more often, as these materials make tunnels very strong.

Engineers have to consider what the tunnel is going to be used for when deciding on the lining. For example, tunnels that will be transporting sewage will need to be lined with a material that can withstand chemicals.

Often, the tunnels are supported with **beams** made of steel and iron. Think of your skeleton. The beams work like the body's bones. They are a way to provide structure and shape to the tunnel, just as your bones do the same for your body.

In the next chapter, we'll look at some different types of tunnels and what they are used for!

? CONSIDER AND DISCUSS

It's time to consider and discuss: What kind of machinery might people invent in the future to do the work of digging tunnels?

STUCK!

What happens if a TBM breaks down underground? In 2013, a TBM named Bertha stopped working in the Alaskan Way Viaduct replacement tunnel under Seattle, Washington. It took workers almost two years to dig down 120 feet to where Bertha was stuck to do repairs! After the boring was finally completed, Bertha was broken up into huge pieces that were removed from the tunnel in 2017.

BEAM STRENGTH

Candy can be used for more than just eating. It can become a beam, like the supports in the entrances and exits of tunnels. Use a scientific method worksheet and this tasty activity to test the strength of beams!

1 Place the taffy beam on top of the two marshmallows. The marshmallows should be evenly spaced, with one supporting the left side of the taffy and the other marshmallow supporting the right side of the taffy.

2 Test your beam! What is its load capacity, or amount it can hold? Put one square of chocolate in the middle of the taffy beam. Stack more chocolate squares on top of the first square until the taffy beam bends into an upside-down arch. Record the number of chocolate squares in your notebook.

3 Remove the chocolate. Turn the beam over and place it on the marshmallows so it now forms an arch. Test out the load capacity again. Can you stack more chocolate onto the center of an arch than you can on a beam? Record the findings in your notebook.

TRY THIS! The top of a tunnel is often an arch. Now you know why! Cut off (or bite off!) some taffy and test the beam again. Then flip it when it becomes an arch. Continue to test the strength of the beam and arch, making the taffy shorter each time. What happens when the taffy gets shorter? Is the arch still stronger than the beam? Record your findings in your notebook.

MAKE A DRILL

Although making a giant drill to bore into the center of the earth would be impossible, you can make your own hand drill!

Caution: Ask an adult to help you with the glue and the drill bits.

1 Take the dowel and file each end of it with the sand paper. This will make it nice and smooth.

2 Push the drill bit into one end of the freshly-sanded dowel. Twist the dowel as you hold the drill bit, so the drill bit enters the wood.

3 If you have pliers, use them to grip the metal bit extra tightly and twist the dowel even harder.

4 Pull the drill bit out. You made a hole in the dowel with the drill side of the drill bit!

5 Flip the drill bit around so the smooth side is ready to be placed into the hole you made.

6 Before you place the bit into the hole, with an adult's help, cover the end of the bit in super-sticky glue.

7   Place the sticky end into the wooden dowel. The drill part is now sticking out! Let the glue dry according to the instructions that come with the glue.

8   Check the strength of your new hand drill by testing it on a piece of scrap wood. Twist your hand drill with the palm of your hand to drill your own small hole—a teeny, tiny tunnel!

TRY THIS! Make more drills using different size dowels and drill bits. Line them up in a box or hang them from a shelf in your garage. You now have a tool kit, filled with drills!

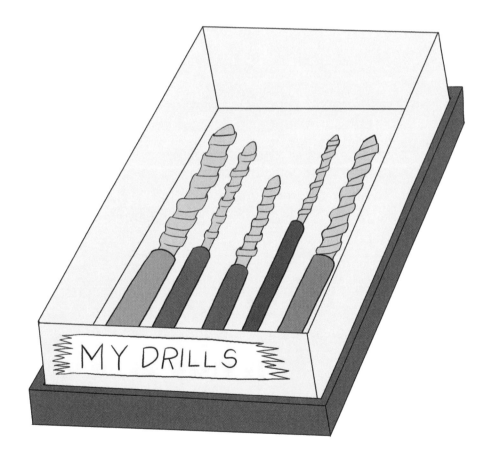

MY DRILLS

MAKE A SIEVE

How do we figure out if a material is made up of big or small pieces? Sand looks small, and gravel looks bigger, but how much bigger? Make yourself a tool needed by engineers and geologists to figure out what is in the soil and how big the particles are.

SUPPLIES

* paper plate or bowl
* nail or fork
* different materials, such as sand, soil, or dirt with pebbles
* engineering notebook and pencil

1 Use the nail or fork to poke holes through the bottom of the plate or bowl. The holes should be the same size. This is your sieve.

2 Place the first type of material into the sieve. Rock it lightly back and forth.

3 What is left in the sieve? Why won't that material go through the sieve? Make some notes in your engineering notebook about the size of the materials.

4 Repeat step 3 with a different type of material. What is left in the sieve this time? What is the difference in the diameter of the first material and the second material?

TRY THIS! Gather more materials and test the sieve. Widen the holes of the sieve to allow other materials to pass through. Make a second sieve with very small holes. What passes through this? Why?

THE HUMAN TUNNEL

The top of a tunnel is often shaped like an arch. An arch has great load capacity, as you have learned. Arches also make it possible for large vehicles—such as trains, trucks, and buses—to pass through. We can form arches and tunnels with our bodies. Grab a few partners!

1 To test out a human arch, face another person. Take two steps back, away from one another. Reach your arms out.

2 Clasp your hands together—left to left and right to right. Bend your heads through the space between your arms. You have a human arch!

3 Repeat steps 1 to 2 with two more people to the right of the first pair. And then with two more people to the left of the first pair.

4 Keep repeating these steps in pairs of two with as many people as you can use.

Now you have a human tunnel! The floor is the bottom of the tunnel. The bodies are the sides and top of the tunnel.

TRY THIS! What can pass through this human tunnel? An adult probably won't be able to crawl through this tunnel! But perhaps a toy dump truck can go right through!

TUNNEL OF SNACKS

Some tunnels are constructed for vehicles to pass through to get from one place to another. Some tunnels are deep within the ground and used for mining precious metals and stones. And other tunnels . . . well, they are good for snackin'! Give this one a try.

1 Lay your materials on a clean surface. This is your work site. Take your plastic knife and dip it into the peanut butter—your concrete!

2 Spread the peanut butter along the edges of two crackers. Link the crackers together. You may need an extra layer to seal these edges.

3 Using more peanut butter, add another cracker to the first two to hold them together. Keep adding crackers until you create an arch. Continue adding crackers to build a tunnel.

4 Measure the diameter of your tunnel with a ruler. What kinds of items can pass through a tunnel with this diameter? List objects in your classroom that could fit.

5 After you finish working with the tunnel, eat it if you want!

THINK ABOUT IT: What difficulties did you have constructing a tunnel out of crackers? What would have made it easier? Start an engineering design worksheet and build a better tunnel.

TUNNEL-MAKING CRITTERS

What kinds of animals live beneath the earth's surface? Many! There are a variety of critters that make tunnels in the soil. They have burrows and networks that lead to their nests. These dwellings provide cozy dens for creatures to rest, sleep, take care of babies, and store food.

1 Choose a type of animal that lives underground. Ideas include a mole, burrow frog, snake, rabbit, or skunk.

2 Research your animal. You can visit the library to find books about it. You can also do research on the internet. Try the National Geographic animal index website for some ideas.

KEYWORD PROMPTS

Nat Geo animals index 🔍

3 Write one page about your animal in your engineering notebook. Describe what it looks like, what it eats, and some of its habits. Draw a picture of your animal in its tunnel environment.

4 Present your findings to your classmates and friends. You might decide to create a poster or a PowerPoint presentation with your information.

TRY THIS! Create a fact list for your animal. Find other animals that are related to your animal or are of the same family. Did you know moles belong to a family called Talpidae? Do some research. You may be surprised!

CHAPTER 4

TYPES OF TUNNELS

• • • • • • • • • • •   • • • • • • • • •

Tunnel construction takes lots of hard work from many different people. They all perform their jobs to make sure that the tunnel they build is safe, well constructed, and even beautiful to look at!

• •

You've learned about the different kinds of engineering techniques and tools that are used to create tunnels. Now let's look at some of the different kinds of tunnels that are built.

There are three main types of tunnels. Engineers must pick one of these types before they can move forward with their plans.

INVESTIGATE!

Why are there different types of tunnels?

cut-and-cover: a tunnel-making technique that involves digging a trench and covering it up.

WORDS to KNOW

CUT-AND-COVER TUNNELS

Cut-and-cover tunnels are made just how their name describes. After the engineers have studied the land and know it is good for making a tunnel, workers create a trench, add in a liner, and then cover up the open part to make the tunnel.

A trench is a long, narrow cut in the ground. It looks like a ditch, but is longer. Trenches can be used for draining the land. They give water a channel to flow through in whatever direction is necessary.

In tunneling, a trench can be the start of the tunnel-digging process. The trenches are sometimes dug by hand with shovels and tools, but more often workers use large machines called excavators.

After the trench is created, a roof is put over the top. This isn't like the roof of a house or a building, though. It is made from materials such as concrete, steel rods, and dirt. The roof of a tunnel must be strong enough to carry the weight that will be on top of the tunnel. Often, the roof is also lined with a shield to prevent rocks or other material from falling onto trains, cars, or people.

Cut-and-cover tunnels come in two different forms. The first is built using the bottom-up method. A trench is dug and the first part of the tunnel is built in that trench. The bottom of the trench is lined with concrete. Upside-down arches made of steel are added to the trench to make the tunnel strong.

DID YOU KNOW?

Hundreds of years ago, concrete was not used. Instead, workers used bricks or even neatly cut rocks to line the bottoms of trenches.

EARTHQUAKE!

You might think that because tunnels are built underground, earthquakes would cause lots of damage to tunnels around the world. However, underground subway systems are often far less damaged during an earthquake than the city that towers above them. The tunnels shift with the **seismic waves** that move through the ground during an earthquake.

The other type of cut-and-cover tunnel is built using the top-down method. In this method, the sides of the trench are constructed so they can support the roof of the tunnel. Then, the top of the tunnel is built before the bottom of the tunnel. This method works well for tunnels that are built under roads.

The cut-and-cover method works best for shallow tunnels, such as underground train stations. The Canary Wharf station in London is a good example. Very long trains can pass through these tunnels. Some of these trains have as many as 10 or 12 cars!

Most of London is linked by a great underground network of train tunnels, called the London Underground. The London Underground used the cut-and-cover technique for many of its tunnels.

ESCALATORS INTO THE CANARY WHARF TUBE STATION

The underground tunnels and stations usually have two levels. One level has an area for purchasing tickets, emergency access, and places where passengers can walk. The air-conditioning and heat systems can be placed in the first level, along with rooms for the staff that work at the train stations. The trains run on the other level.

BORED TUNNELS

Bored tunnels are made with the tunnel boring machines (TBMs) that you learned about in Chapter 3. A TBM drills its way through the dirt and leaves a passageway behind. One advantage of TBMs is that they can dig under cities without causing major disruptions to life overhead. There might be a bored tunnel being dug beneath you right now!

THE LONDON UNDERGROUND

The London Underground has been known as the "Tube" since 1890. The name comes from the shape of its tunnels. The London Underground is a very fast underground transit system that brings people to different points around the city of London. It was the world's first underground railway. When it was first created, the engineers used the cut-and-cover method. Years later, engineers constructed deeper tunnels.

PS Take a lesson on how to get around via the Tube at this website!

KEYWORD PROMPTS

travel better underground

IMMERSED TUBE TUNNELS

Sometimes, tunnels are constructed underwater. The Channel Tunnel linking England and France is a famous example of an underwater tunnel that you'll learn more about in Chapter 5.

Engineers build immersed-tube tunnels underwater for people and vehicles to travel through. The tubes are built in large sections on dry land. Then, these sections of tube are floated into the water and placed in a trench-bed that was dug beforehand.

The tubes are settled into position and joined together to make the tunnel. The trench gets filled in around the tubes and the underwater surface goes back to its normal level.

immersed-tube tunnel: a tunnel that lies beneath the bottom of a body of water.

ground disturbance: a disturbance on the surface of the earth, such as an earthquake.

WORDS TO KNOW

DID YOU KNOW?

The word *immersed* means surrounded by. An immersed-tube tunnel is made of tubes surrounded by water.

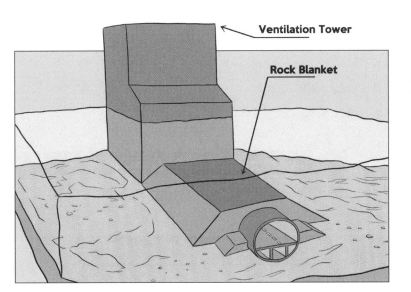
Ventilation Tower

Rock Blanket

Immersed tunnels cause very little ground disturbance, but they can be more expensive than above-ground projects. And sometimes, they end up costing far more than planned!

deteriorate: to break down and collapse or lose pieces.

monitor: to watch carefully.

WORDS ⊙ KNOW

But, immersed-tube tunnels often provide great solutions to transporting people and goods. An immersed-tube tunnel—the Fehmarn Belt Fixed Link—is planned to connect Denmark and Germany through the Baltic Sea some day!

TRICKY TUNNELING

Sometimes, the materials in tunnels **deteriorate**, or start to get old and start to break down. Leaks can occur, especially between the joints where the tops of the tubes meet the bottoms of the tubes. Materials can also shrink and expand because of changes in temperature around a tunnel, and these tiny movements can eventually cause more damage.

Tunnels are **monitored** and inspected by experts. They know what to look for before damage can become a problem for people using the tunnel!

Now that you know all about the engineering and design that goes into planning and digging tunnels, let's take a look at some famous tunnels from around the world! Maybe you have been to some of these tunnels!

WHY COULD THE TRAIN CONDUCTOR FOCUS?

HA HA HA

He had tunnel vision!

? CONSIDER AND DISCUSS

It's time to consider and discuss: Why are there different types of tunnels?

PROJECT!

MAKE YOUR OWN CONCRETE

Concrete is an important building material used in tunnel construction. It is sturdy and made of three basic things: water, aggregate, and cement. Aggregate is a mix of sand, rock, and gravel. Cement is lime powder and clay. When aggregate and cement are mixed with water, the resulting concrete hardens and joins objects together. The concrete binds like glue!

1 Put the flour and water into the bowl. Stir the flour and water with a spoon until there are no lumps. Stir in the salt. This prevents **mold** from growing.

2 Use this "cement"—called papier-mâché—in the next activity!

TRY THIS! Consider where you live. If you live in a **humid** area of the world, you will want to use slightly less water in cement than someone who lives in an area that is not humid at all.

Research humidity and why it would affect making papier-mâché. **Check out this website and video on humidity.**

KEYWORD PROMPTS

National Geographic humidity 🔍

WORDS ⊙ **KNOW**

mold: a furry growth.

humid: having a high level of moisture in the air.

CEMENT TUNNEL IN TWO PIECES

The cut-and-cover method deals with two parts of the tunnel: the bottom and the top. You can use this tunneling method even without a giant boring machine!

SUPPLIES

* papier-mâché glue from the last activity
* strips of newspaper
* empty plastic bottle
* plastic knife

1 Take some of the papier-mâché glue and spread it on the strips of newspaper so you can make a structure.

2 Lay the glued pieces of newspaper over an object, such as the empty plastic bottle. Put overlapping layers all over one side of the object in many different directions to completely cover half of it.

3 Wait for the glued newspaper to dry and then use the plastic knife to pry it away from the bottle, being careful not to break the paper. You now have half of a tube or tunnel. This can be the roof of your tunnel.

4 Repeat steps 1–3 to create the bottom of the tunnel.

5 Use more strips of newspaper and more papier-mâché to glue the two pieces of tunnel together to form a tube. You have a papier-mâché tunnel!

TRY THIS! Use acrylic paints to give your tunnel a makeover. Color it gray so it looks like cement. Or add designs to it so it looks creative and different!

PROJECT!

DIGGING FOR FACTS

SUPPLIES

✳ internet access
✳ engineering notebook and pencil

Research is an important part of what engineers do. They need to understand the area where a tunnel is needed to properly plan a safe design. Put on your researcher glasses and get ready to find out about amazing tunnels in the world.

1 Create a chart in your notebook that looks like this.

Tunnel Name	Location	Length	History

Diagram of _____:

2 With an adult's permission, go to the following website to find information about some amazing tunnels. Select a few that you find interesting! Record your findings in the chart in your notebook.

KEYWORD PROMPTS

20 most impressive tunnels 🔍

3 Share your tunnel research with your classmates or a partner. Did other people also find your tunnels to be fascinating? Discuss the tunnels with your classmates or your partner.

TRY THIS! In your notebook, create another chart like the one before. This time, research tunnels from long ago. Here is a good place to start.

KEYWORD PROMPTS

Roman aqueducts Kids Discover tunnels 🔍

PROJECT!

EARTHQUAKE!

SUPPLIES

* an adult to help
* cardboard box
* nail or ice pick
* string
* paper clips

Earthquakes can move the earth at any time. They can also move structures such as houses, buildings, bridges, and tunnels. Earthquakes create waves. These seismic waves travel through many materials as they move away from the epicenter, or source, of the earthquake.

> **Caution:** An adult must help with cutting the box and with using the nail or ice pick.

1 Remove one side of the box. An adult can help you with a box cutter. Also with an adult's help, punch holes in the top and bottom of the box using a nail or ice pick.

2 Thread a string so it runs from the top to the bottom of the box. Tie it off on the bottom. At the top, tie the string to a paper clip outside the box. Be sure the string is not loose. Place four or five paper clips on the string inside the box.

3 Place the box on a table that you can hit to make it **vibrate**. Hit the table hard enough to make energy waves move through the table. If you hit the table hard enough, the paper clips will start to move and shake.

4 Place the box on a different surface, such as the floor. Try to make the box vibrate.

WORDS to KNOW

epicenter: the point on the earth's crust where an earthquake starts.

vibrate: to move back and forth quickly.

68

5 Test the box on different surfaces and compare how the energy waves travel through the box on each.

TRY THIS! Replace the string with dental floss, thick yarn, or fishing wire. Does this make any difference in how the energy travels when you hit the surface? Or is it just the hitting of the surface that helps the energy travel? You decide!

SMACK

TRENCH MAKING

Trenches have been dug for centuries. They were used to irrigate fields to grow crops more efficiently. They were even used during war times. Trenches provided hiding spots and shelter for soldiers. As you learned earlier, trenches are also the first step in the cut-and-cover method of tunneling.

SUPPLIES

* backyard or area with sand or loose soil
* small shovel or large spoon
* ruler
* small pebbles and sand
* pail of water

1 Locate a flat spot full of sand and dirt for your trench. Ask an adult if you can dig there! Use your spoon or shovel to dig a small, narrow area to make a shallow trench, about 12 to 24 inches long. As you dig, use your ruler to measure the trench until it is 2 inches deep.

2 Start to angle your trench by making the right side slightly deeper than the left. The right side of the trench should be 3 inches deep and the left side should be 2 inches deep. Measure with your ruler.

3 Take your small pebbles and line the entire bottom of the trench with them. Pack the pebbles tightly. Seal the cracks between the pebbles with sand. This acts as a filler, almost like cement.

4 Pour some water into the trench to test it. Does the water flow from left to right as you pour it? Repair areas where the water soaks through with more pebbles and sand and try again.

TRY THIS! Line the trench with strips of newspaper glued together with papier-mâché to make the bottom of the trench stronger. Test the trench with water again. Does it hold better?

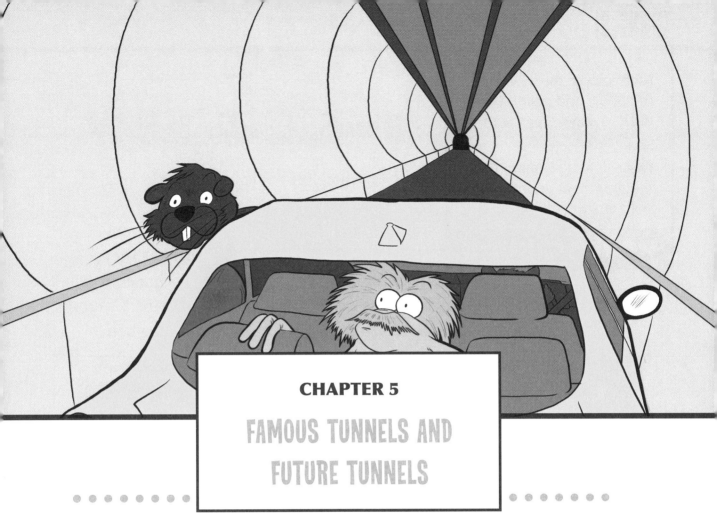

CHAPTER 5

FAMOUS TUNNELS AND FUTURE TUNNELS

People have been digging tunnels for thousands of years. Ancient tunnels were used for many of the same purposes as today's tunnels—transportation of people and items, the movement of water, mining, and travel. Without tunnels, the world might be a very different place!

Today, some ancient tunnels are still in use, and engineers are designing new ways to build stronger, more reliable tunnels every day. Let's look at some of the most famous tunnels in the world. Maybe you've traveled through one of these before!

INVESTIGATE!

What kinds of **technology** will future generations use to dig tunnels?

TUNNELS!

technology: the tools, methods, and systems used to solve a problem or do work.

feat: an achievement that requires great courage, skill, or strength.

WORDS TO KNOW

THE CHANNEL TUNNEL

The Channel Tunnel connects Folkstone, Kent, in the United Kingdom, with Pas-de-Calais in northern France. Going under the English Channel, this tunnel has the longest undersea section of any tunnel in the world—23.5 miles. Trains carry passengers, cars, trucks, and other vehicles through the tunnel—at up to 99 miles per hour!

It is an amazing construction project and very successful, but it wasn't a new idea. A French engineer named Albert Mathieu thought there should be a tunnel built under the English Channel way back in 1802! Both English and French workers came together to create this amazing **feat** of engineering.

> **DID YOU KNOW?**
> The Laerdal Tunnel is the only tunnel in the world that includes its own air treatment plant!

A CAR ENTERING A TRAIN FOR THE CHANNEL TUNNEL

THE LAERDAL TUNNEL

The Laerdal Tunnel, located in Norway, is the world's longest road tunnel at 15.2 miles. And it cost $153 million!

psychologist: a specialist who studies the mind and behavior and provides mental health care.

claustrophobia: a fear of confined spaces.

WORDS TO KNOW

The tunnel takes 20 minutes to drive through, so psychologists put their heads together with engineers to figure out how to make traveling the tunnel more pleasant. Engineers used different design features to help travelers with claustrophobia so they could travel through the tunnel without problems.

One technique they came up with was to separate the tunnel into different sections so drivers can take quick breaks or stop if they need to rest. The tunnel is also colorfully lit.

INSIDE THE LAERDAL TUNNEL

WORDS **TO** **KNOW**

bamboo: a type of tropical grass that resembles a tree. Its wood is hollow and solid and it can grow extremely quickly, up to a couple of feet per day!

WORDS TO KNOW

THE EISENHOWER TUNNEL

The Eisenhower Tunnel in Colorado in the United States is the world's highest road tunnel at 11,158 feet above sea level. It is the highest point of the United States' interstate highway system, too.

Its height isn't this tunnel's only claim to fame. The Eisenhower Tunnel was also very important to the women's rights movement. In 1972, Janet Bonnema (1938–2008) was hired as an engineering technician because her supervisor thought her name was James! He misread it on the application.

WHAT DID THE CONCRETE SAY TO THE BULLDOZER?

HA HA HA

You crack me up!

THROUGH THE BAMBOO

There is a beautiful natural tunnel in Kyoto, Japan. It is made of **bamboo** shoots. This area of Japan is known for its groves of bamboo, and in some of these groves, narrow paths are surrounded by bamboo plants that soar overhead.

When he discovered she was a woman, the supervisor decided to give her administrative work instead of letting her work in the tunnels. Discrimination against women was common then, and many workers thought a woman working in the tunnel would bring bad luck.

> **discrimination:** to deny a group of people opportunities based on things such as race or gender.
>
> **amend:** to change a law.
>
> **WORDS TO KNOW**

Bonnema sued the company, and voters in Colorado agreed to amend the state constitution to guarantee equal rights for women. Bonnema was finally allowed to enter the tunnel to do her work.

Do you think this kind of discrimination could happen in today's world?

THE EISENHOWER TUNNEL

(CREDIT: BENJAMIN CLARK)

THE FUTURE OF TUNNELS

One project on the horizon is interesting to both engineers and archaeologists. A tunnel is planned around Stonehenge, one of the most famous landmarks in the world!

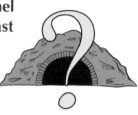

Stonehenge is a ring of standing stones in England that archaeologists believe were placed between 3000 and 2000 BCE. A lot of traffic on a very busy road runs near the stones, which makes this popular tourist destination noisy and hard to get to.

In 2017, the U.K. government approved the idea of a tunnel around Stonehenge. Many people—especially archeologists—have been opposed. Digging in an area of great historical significance can be tricky.

(CREDIT: A.J. BUTLER)

What if the TBM hits something important? Archaeologists and engineers are now trying to work together to make this a successful project without hurting any of the artifacts found around Stonehenge.

Inventor Elon Musk—known for Tesla electric cars—is proposing another kind of tunnel. He has been thinking about solutions to traffic problems in big cities. One of his ideas is a high-speed network of tunnels!

FAMOUS NATURAL TUNNELS

The Oak Alley **Plantation** in Louisiana is known for its long line of oak trees that swoop over to form a tunnel. These trees were planted in the 1700s along a road that leads right to the plantation. The tunnel of trees is so famous, it has even been used in movies!

Cars could be transported down from the road by a kind of elevator and moved to different exits at very high speeds by a fully automated system. Sound exciting? His company, the Boring Co., is currently starting to build tunnels under Los Angeles, California. This might be the future of road tunnels!

As the population expands, we'll see more tunnels being built to make travel easier for both people and things. Just as we no longer dig tunnels by hand as people did in ancient times, future generations might not use the machines we think of as cutting edge, such as the EPBM, in the future.

Although we don't know what kind of tunnels the future will bring, we can be pretty sure that tunnels will always be a part of the landscape in which we live.

CONSIDER AND DISCUSS

It's time to consider and discuss: What kinds of technology will future generations use to dig tunnels?

You can see videos of what a high-speed tunnel system might look like at this website.

KEYWORD PROMPTS

Verge Boring

SUPPLIES

* engineering notebook and pencil
* magnifying glass
* partner

TUNNELS EVERYWHERE

Tunnels can be in houses or buildings. They can also occur in nature right beneath our feet. In this activity, you can use your scavenging skills and locate tunnels in your town or city.

1 Look for tunnels in your building or home first. Is there a crawl space in the attic? A central air system in the school?

2 Make a chart in your notebook and record your findings.

Location	Type of Tunnel	Used For	Diagram

3 Step outside. Use the magnifying glass to investigate possible animal or bug tunnels. Ant hills, mole tunnels, chipmunk tunnels—the creatures outside make tunnels, too! Add them to the list.

4 Share your findings with your partner. Did your partner find some tunnels that you did not? Add them to your chart!

TRY THIS! Make a map of your yard or a local park. Locate the tunnels on your map, along with important landmarks. Can your partner use your map to find all the tunnels?

SUPPLIES

* *The Tunnel* by Anthony Browne
* engineering notebook and pencil

LITERATURE CONNECTION

Civil engineers must read many books if they are ever going to build tunnels successfully! But tunnels also appear in kids' books on our library shelves. Peek into the pages of one book about a tunnel.

1 Listen to the book *The Tunnel* by Anthony Browne or get the book from the library and read it. You can find a reading of *The Tunnel* at this website.

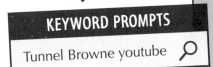

KEYWORD PROMPTS

Tunnel Browne youtube

2 Why does the sister, Rose, find the tunnel frightening? Do you ever feel fear or claustrophobia when you go into tunnels or even think about tunnels?

3 How are the brother and sister different from each other? Do you have a brother or sister? Are you very different or are you similar?

4 How does Rose overcome her fear of the tunnel?

5 Write a new story in your notebook with the same title. Who are the characters in your story? Where does the tunnel in your story lead to?

TRY THIS! Choose one of the tunnels discussed in this book and write about it. Describe what it looks like. Where does it lead to? Write an adventure story that involves this tunnel.

SUPPLIES

* notebook or tracing paper
* pencil

MAP MAKING

Geologists are key players in the world of tunnel design. They investigate the land where a tunnel is planned, produce reports about the land, and even take part in the digging. They understand the soil very well, and often have to use maps to figure out the location of different places. Now it's your turn!

1 Locate a map of your town or community. Find different areas on the map that could benefit from a tunnel. Perhaps there are two streets where people always get stuck in traffic—an underground tunnel might help! Is there a railroad line that could use a tunnel?

2 Design your own map. It can be like the one you are studying. You can use the tracing paper to copy the map you are using.

3 Use the symbols on this website and put them in your map. Notice the symbol for tunnels in the "Roads and Related Features" section. Put it in your drawing.

4 Add color to your map. You are now a geologist in training!

KEYWORD PROMPTS

map symbols compass dude 🔍

TRY THIS! Take another piece of tracing paper. Add another layer to your map on this second piece of paper. For example, you could include bridges at intersections so people can cross roads easily, lakes in parks, or gardens for the community. Get creative!

SUPPLIES

❋ engineering notebook and pencil

TUNNELS AND REAL-WORLD PROBLEM SOLVING

The National Academy of Engineering has issued 14 challenges for the twenty-first century. These challenges ask student to think like engineers and come up with solutions to real-life problems. You can browse the National Academy of Engineering challenges at this website.

1 Consider this challenge from the National Academy of Engineering: "Provide access to clean water." Take a moment to think about what that means. What parts of the world are lacking in clean water? What is the geography like there? What are some ways to get clean water to people who need it?

KEYWORD PROMPTS

NAE challenges 🔍

2 Think about how clean water problems relate to tunnels. What can tunnels do to provide people access to fresh, clean water? What kind of invention might help?

3 Talk about your ideas with a friend and record your ideas in your notebook. Prepare a presentation of your ideas and share it with the class.

TRY THIS! Another challenge has to do with restoring and improving urban infrastructure. Research what urban infrastructure is. How can tunneling help improve urban areas? Write down your ideas in your engineering notebook.

SUPPLIES

✳ engineering notebook and pencil

VOCABULARY SKILLS: PREFIXES!

Many words in the English language have prefixes. Prefixes are parts of words that are attached to root words to create the definitions. Even the word *prefix* has a prefix! *Pre-* is a prefix that means "before." Many construction words have prefixes. Let's take a look.

1 Create a grid that has four columns and six rows, like the one shown here.

	Prefix	Root and Suffix	Definition
REcessed			
UNstable			
INvestigate			
SUBway			
UNDERpass			

2 List these five words in the first row: epicenter, aqueduct, investigate, subway, and geological.

3 In the prefix column, write the prefix of each word. In the root column, write the root word.

4 Look up the definition of each word. Write it in the last column.

5 Use a dictionary to find the definition of each prefix. How is each prefix related to the definition of each word?

TRY THIS! Add five more rows. Find five more words in this book with prefixes and add them to your table. Where else can you find words with prefixes?

air pressure: the weight of air that is pressing down on the earth.

amend: to change a law.

aqueduct: a channel that transports water from its source over a great distance.

arch: a curved structure in the shape of an upside-down U.

archaeologist: a scientist who studies ancient people through the objects they left behind.

artifact: an object, such as a tool, that was made in the past.

automated: controlled by a computer instead of by a person.

bamboo: a type of tropical grass that resembles a tree. Its wood is hollow and solid and it can grow extremely quickly, up to a couple of feet per day!

BCE: put after a date, BCE stands for Before Common Era and counts down to zero. CE stands for Common Era and counts up from zero. This book was printed in 2018 CE.

beam: a rigid, horizontal structure that carries a load.

bench: in top-heading-and-bench construction, the area that is excavated below the heading.

blasting: removing rocks and materials with the use of explosives.

burrow: to dig an underground hole or tunnel.

canal: a manmade waterway built for shipping, navigation, or irrigation.

cavern: a cave, especially one that is large and mostly underground.

cement: lime powder and clay mixed with water that hardens and joins objects together.

characteristic: a feature of a person, place, or thing.

civil engineer: someone who designs structures such as public roads, bridges, buildings, and tunnels.

claustrophobia: a fear of confined spaces.

coal: a dark brown or black rock formed from decayed plants. Coal is a fossil fuel.

coarse: composed of large particles.

cohesive: holding together firmly or stickily.

collapse: to fall in or down suddenly.

compression: a pushing force that squeezes or presses material inward.

concrete: a construction material made with cement, sand, and water that hardens.

congestion: when something is filled to excess, crowded, or overburdened.

cut-and-cover: a tunnel-making technique that involves digging a trench and covering it up.

cylinder: a hollow tube shape.

data: information, facts, and numbers from tests and experiments.

density: a measure of how closely packed items are.

destination: the place to which someone or something is going.

deteriorate: to break down and collapse or lose pieces.

detonate: to explode or cause to explode.

diameter: the distance across a circle through the middle.

discrimination: to deny a group of people opportunities based on things such as race or gender.

drafting engineer: an engineer who plans projects and creates models.

earth pressure balance machine (EPBM): a large machine that bores through soft ground and uses the excavated material to support the tunnel walls.

earthquake: a sudden movement in pieces of the outer layer of the earth.

echo: a sound caused by the reflection of sound waves from a surface back to the listener.

efficient: wasting as little time or effort as possible when completing a task.

electrical engineer: an engineer who designs systems and processes that use electricity.

engineer: a person who uses science, math, and creativity to design and build things.

epicenter: the point on the earth's crust where an earthquake starts.

equipment operator: someone who uses heavy equipment when working on a construction site.

excavate: to dig a hole or channel in the ground, or to make a hole by removing earth.

explosive: a substance that is used to blow up structures.

feat: an achievement that requires great courage, skill, or strength.

fire-setting: the process of using fire and water to soften and crack rock.

force: a push or a pull that causes a change of motion in an object.

fossil fuels: coal, oil, and natural gas. These non-renewable energy sources come from the fossils of plants and tiny animals that lived millions of years ago.

fossil: the remains or traces of ancient plants or animals.

full-face: a method of constructing tunnels that involves digging the entire diameter of the tunnel at the same time.

geologist: a scientist who studies geology, which is the history and structure of Earth and its rocks.

geotechnical engineer: an engineer who studies the earth and its rocks.

grain size: the size of clay, silt, or sand particles.

ground disturbance: a disturbance on the surface of the earth, such as an earthquake.

hazard: a danger or risk.

heading: in top-heading-and-bench construction, a small tunnel that is the start of a larger tunnel.

hollow: having a hole or empty space inside.

humid: having a high level of moisture in the air.

igneous rock: rock that forms from cooling magma.

immersed-tube tunnel: a tunnel that lies beneath the bottom of a body of water.

incline: a slope, especially on a road or railway.

infrastructure: roads, bridges, and other basic types of structures and equipment needed for a country to function properly.

innovate: to come up with a new way of doing something.

irrigate: to supply land with water so that crops and plants will grow.

length: the measurement of something from end to end.

limestone: a sedimentary rock that forms from the skeletons and shells of sea creatures.

magma: hot, melted rock below the surface of the earth.

matter: what an object is made of.

metamorphic rock: rock that has been transformed by heat or pressure or both into new rock, while staying solid.

mineral: a naturally occurring solid found in rocks and in the ground. Rocks are made of minerals. Gold and diamonds are precious minerals.

mold: a furry growth.

monitor: to watch carefully.

muck: material removed during the process of excavating.

natural resource: something from nature that people can use in some way, such as water, stone, and wood.

obstacle: something that blocks your way.

particle: a tiny piece of matter.

physics: the science of how matter and energy work together.

plantation: a large farm in a hot climate. In colonial times, plantations used slaves as workers.

prototype: a model of something that allows engineers to test their ideas.

psychologist: a specialist who studies the mind and behavior and provides mental health care.

ratio: the relationship in size or quantity between two or more things.

reflection: when light or sound hits an object and bounces off it.

regulations: rules that engineers need to follow when designing and building a project.

reservoir: a manmade or natural lake used to collect water that can be stored for future use.

sedimentary rock: rock formed from the compression of sediments, the remains of plants and animals, or the evaporation of seawater.

seismic wave: energy waves from within the earth.

sensor: a device that takes measurements and gives a computer information about its surroundings.

sewer: a drain for wastewater.

shear: a sliding force that slips parts of a material in opposite directions.

sieve: a tool that is used for separating coarse material from fine material.

silt: soil made up of fine bits of rock.

soil auger: an instrument that drills into the ground so scientists can test the soil.

split-spoon sampler: a tool for measuring the density of soil.

stand-up time: the amount of time the walls of a tunnel can stand unsupported.

technology: the tools, methods, and systems used to solve a problem or do work.

tension: a pulling force that pulls or stretches an object.

texture: a classification of soil.

thermal: related to heat.

tomb: a room or place where a dead person is buried.

top-heading-and-bench: a method of constructing tunnels that involves digging layers of the tunnel from the top down.

torsion: a twisting force.

transport: to move goods or people from one place to another.

trench: a ditch dug into the ground.

tunnel: a passageway that goes through or under natural or manmade obstacles, such as rivers, mountains, roads, and buildings.

tunnel boring machine (TBM): a large machine with a drill in the front that can bore holes through hard rock to make tunnels.

vibrate: to move back and forth quickly.

METRIC CONVERSIONS

Use this chart to find the metric equivalents to the English measurements in this book. If you need to know a half measurement, divide by two. If you need to know twice the measurement, multiply by two. How do you find a quarter measurement? How do you find three times the measurement?

English	Metric
1 inch	2.5 centimeters
1 foot	30.5 centimeters
1 yard	0.9 meter
1 mile	1.6 kilometers
1 pound	0.5 kilogram
1 teaspoon	5 milliliters
1 tablespoon	15 milliliters
1 cup	237 milliliters

BOOKS

Latham, Donna. *Bridges and Tunnels: Investigate Feats of Engineering with 25 Projects* (Build It Yourself). Nomad Press, May 2012.

Nardo, Don. Building *History: Roman Roads and Aqueducts (Building History)*. Lucent Books, September 2000.

Bell, Samantha S. *Building Tunnels (Engineer Challenges)*. Focus Readers, August 2017.

Parker, Steven. *I Wonder Why Tunnels Are Round: and Other Questions About Building.* Kingfisher, September 1995.

Donovan, Sandra. *The Channel Tunnel (Great Building Feats)*. Lerner Pub Group, January 2003.

Bayley, Stephen. *Work: The Building of the Channel Tunnel Rail Link.* Merrell Pub Ltd., July 2008.

McCosker, Mary, and Mary Solon. *Building the Caldecott Tunnel (Images of America)*. Arcadia Publishing, September 2014.

Wolny, Philip. *High-Risk Construction Work: Life Building Skyscrapers, Bridges, and Tunnels (Extreme Careers)*. Rosen Central, September 2008.

Landau, Elaine. *Tunnels (True Books: Buildings and Structures)*. Children's Press, May 2001.

Baby Professor. *Building Landmarks: Bridges, Tunnels and Buildings.* Baby Professor, December 2017.

Mackay, Donald A. *The Building of Manhattan*. Holt McDougal, April 2010.

Kenney, Karen Latchana. *Building a Tunnel (Sequencing Amazing Structures)*. Amicus Ink, August 2018.

Richards, Jon. *It'll Never Work: An Accidental History of Inventions – Bridges and Tunnels.* Franklin Watts, January 2018.

VIDEOS

PBS: Building the Channel Tunnel
vermont.pbslearningmedia.org/resource/
phy03.sci.phys.mfw.bbchunnel/building-the-channel-tunnel

Washington State Department of Transportation: video collection
wsdot.wa.gov/Projects/Viaduct/Library/Videos

Today in History: Building the Lincoln Tunnel
youtube.com/watch?v=vlJiZ58y8JE

QR CODE GLOSSARY

Page 7: vimeo.com/53745457

Page 19: youtube.com/
watch?v=GzJnOrr5RUE

Page 22: printablepaper.net/
category/graph

Page 47: theverge.com/
2017/12/5/16737488/
boring-company-los-
angeles-map-tunnels

Page 57: nationalgeographic.com/
animals/index

Page 62: youtube.com/
watch?v=thV8xUWohN4

Page 65: nationalgeographic.org/
encyclopedia/humidity

Page 67: popularmechanics.com/
technology/infrastructure/g2559/the-
worlds-20-most-impressive-tunnels

Page 67: kidsdiscover.com/quick-reads/
roman-aqueducts-dawn-plumbing

Page 78: theverge.com/
2017/4/28/15476268/
elon-musk-the-boring-company-
car-tunnel-concept-video

Page 80: youtube.com/
watch?v=ps2E5yoRsMk

Page 81: compassdude.com/
map-symbols.php

Page 82: engineeringchallenges.org/
challenges.aspx

ESSENTIAL QUESTIONS

Introduction: Why are tunnels useful in big cities where there are lots of people?

Chapter 1: What are some of the reasons people need tunnels?

Chapter 2: Why are there different methods of building different tunnels?

Chapter 3: What kind of machinery might people invent
in the future to do the work of digging tunnels?

Chapter 4: Why are there different types of tunnels?

Chapter 5: What kinds of technology will future generations use to dig tunnels?